Steady Hands:
Odes to our Fathers

Austie M. Baird
-Editor, Cover Artist-

Austie M. Baird is a born and raised Oregonian, holding both History and Education degrees from Eastern Oregon University. Long before becoming a wife and mother, Baird connected with the power of the written word, finding healing properties in both reading and writing. She draws strength from the beauty that surrounds her and the overwhelming love of her family.

A.B.Baird Publishing
Oregon, USA

A.B.Baird Publishing
66548 Highway 203
La Grande OR, 97850
USA

www.abbairdpublishing.com

-Table of Contents-

-Table of Contents-

-Table of Contents-

-Authors-

Work from the following authors can be found in the pages of this book.
These 28 authors represent sons and daughters from around the world.
To learn more about each author please visit them on their main writing
platforms on Instagram. For a list of which pages to find each of your
favorites, please visit the index at the back of the book.

Abeer A. Zayyad	@a_scarlet_b
Ambica Gossain	@tryst_with_fiction
Austie M. Baird	@glass_walls_life
Bettie Shade	@bettie_schade
Crystal Nicole	@author_crystalnicole
David Bentata	
Debjeet Mukherjee	@authordebjeet
Eloise	@eloise_the_typewriter
Heini Talip	@missfinnpoet
J. Savarese	@borgo_savarese
Kathleen	@kathleenflavia49
Kevin Vargo	@kevinvargo_
L.T. Pelle	@L.T.Pelle
Lacie Wright	@cowgirllaw
Lara Decastecker	@laradraemi
Lesley Worthington	@worthywrites
LiAnnah Jameson	@liannahjameson
Linda Lokhee	@lindalokheeauthor
M.R.S.	@mrs_poems
Maya Elphick	@m.g.petri
Miriam Otto	@miriamo77

Rhonda Simard	@just26littleletters
Robert Malka	@malkarobert
Russell Willis	russell.willis.1217- Facebook
Sarah Herrin	@_SarahHerrin
Steve Gonzales Jr	@iamwhoiamisme
Will Berry	@theberrycollective
Zan	@farzzu

Memories

Day of Rest

In the thick sunlight of
Sunday evenings,
our throats coated with church bells
and dandelion dust—
we laughed at things like napkins flying
while we ate our dinners outside.
Father, how your firm hands collected them
like flowers
from the wind.
Father, how the day of rest
meant we got the rest of you.

-L.T.Pelle-

Complexity

I still crave it
The secondhand smoke of childhood
Inhale, exhale
Breathe
That time
Before I knew where I was going
Or even who I was
When all I wanted
Was to make him proud
And go on drives
Daddy's girl
Have him test me on times tables
And show him my straight As
Racing to the front door
To see what he brought
To atone for his absence
Or other things
All forgiven
In the sweetness of a favourite chocolate bar
Flavours so complex

- Lesley Worthington-

The Midnight Train

I subsisted on rationed visits of my father's stratus cloud of coffee, cologne and cigarettes,

that wafted in at intervals to replenish the often dwindling reserve of his bottled essence that mother adorned on the corner shelf.

Our rooted memories borne of a drive by tragedy, he and I would persist in watching the night move to kiss dawn with figments and fairytales of love that had lingered;

before too soon goodbyes took his midnight train back along blank maps to hometown strangers.

We made the most of these scheduled moments of uncertainty, basking in the beauty of their let go, despite the weight of their eviscerating ache.

Answering to the call for lost souls, we found redemption repeatedly in sentimental stirrings on reefs and wrecks, that were the only sanctuaries we could call our own;

where we loved enough in short bursts to etch our photographic legacies in notes of sweet nostalgia.

-Ambica Gossain-

So Much Adventure

you always knew that
we could make something of this
and it didn't have to be miserable
because we had six strings on repeat
in an unreliable car
singing Pulp and
speaking in fluent typewriter
pink sunsets
pressed into our cheeks
rosy like our blistered heels
because we've always been running
and yet we never feel
tired
just restless
and wild
and full of heartbeats
that don't belong to us
we knew we could make something of this
but never expected so much adventure

-Maya Elphick-

Father-Braided Hair

Her feet rose off the pedals,
waiting for the mountain
to tell her the secret of exhales
resembling this much beauty,
something you can hold onto,
wildflowers woven through bike spokes
and father-braided hair...

-Eloise-

Deep South, Deep Roots

Fried chicken and biscuits
Southern sweet tea
Warm summer evening
Golden sun stretches through the pines.

Fresh slice of key lime pie
Bowl of butter pecan cream
Crickets chirp-chirp
Harvest moon smiles over the farm.

-Sarah Herrin-

Moon Ladder

We gaze at the sky,
my daddy and I,
from our very own planetarium.

When it is time for bed,
we take a trip instead,
an excursion of the imagination.

Winking and blinking,
the sparkling stars shine.

Warm and inspiring,
my dad's eyes meet mine.
Let's climb, shall we? He asks of me.
I answer, Oh, yes! with a smile.

Grab the moon ladder,
hand over hand,
mile after make believe mile.
Are we there yet? He asks.
Almost... I gasp.

Upward and onward we soar,
a million miles, maybe more.

When at last we arrive,
our night journey survived,
we hang and swing weightlessly...

Wayfarers wondering
whimsically...

What happens when one
hand is set free? Whee!
When both hands let go? Whoaa!

A tumbling descent,
falling stars, whirling wiggles.
A rumbling bed and echoing giggles.

Another nighttime game gone by,
a memory we'll keep.
A dad who helps me reach the sky.
Good night...sweet dreams...to sleep.

-Rhonda Simard-

Dodgem Daddy

Cocooned in the car with her Dad
he and her, seatbelts tugging tight
"Sweetheart," he says, "ready to zoom?"
Heart beating, excitement, feeling light

Music, bells ring, pedal ready?
It's a glorious go and Smash!
Dodgems! Got 'em, spare me please - BUMP!
Memories of childhood love, coming back in a flash!

-Linda Lokhee-

My Dad, His Belief

Evenings spent with dad are lovely for me,
No one wants to miss our family time free.
Mom prepares tea, the best she can choose
While me and dad watches the 6pm news.

Our weekdays are busy, weekends are fun.
Dad loves food, me an ally, mom not-so-much.
I remember fights with him, during my teens;
No beating from him as a kid there has been!

Despite his autumn, pretty young he looks,
Adventure loving guy in mountains and books.
I'll never forget, some of his early teachings.
I treasure those in mind like golden preachings:

"Bring home a smile, when someone is gifting,
The toy maybe broken but keep on smiling.
It's good to get hurt and believe in men,
Than live in mistrust, not to get hurt again!"

Kindergarten notebooks, old photos he keeps;
Safe in cupboard, my childhood memories deep!
I hope I always love my dad, he loves me too;
It's not perfect but we must what we can do.

The best memory is his satisfied pretty look
When he tried reading my first poetry book;
Poems were sorted with time, season and scene,
But dad always kept reading those aged 14!

-Debjeet Mukherjee-

<u>Wolves</u>

I think of me and you
standing out in the black
with a telescope that turns stars
into the stones on our driveway.
I think of wolves chasing clouds
up mountains
and howling at the top
as rain drips down their faces.
I think of foot-tapping in pubs
and giggling in tents
and picnics in castles
and nights we've spent
talking like these days will last forever.
And Dad,
I promise that they will
whenever we're together.

-Maya Elphick-

My Granddaddy

Safety found in a hug scented of leather and Havana Club.
Tenderness in a gravelly voice welcoming me to stay longer and then longer still.
Gentleness found in tanned callouses that pat my cheek and send me back outside to play.
You were larger than life:
Leaving your mark on my 9-year-old heart
Showing me the strongest men are soft.

-Lacie Wright-

Fathers Are

Fathers are the arms you fall into,
when at the age of three you get stuck on the yellow monkey bars.

Fathers are the hands that hold you steady,
as you first learn to peddle down that road- training-wheel-free.

Fathers are the shoulders that carry you,
when crowds get to thick and you cannot see.

Fathers are the chests that you lean on,
when young heart break and tears stream down your face.

Fathers are the ears that you lash on,
when your world spins out of place.

And fathers are the arms that walk you down aisles,
willingly setting you free.

-Austie M. Baird-

This Is Us

My dad may not be Jack Pearson
He may not have built me a model
Of the stadium for the Pittsburgh Steelers
Or taken me for banana pudding ice cream

I watch "This Is Us" and I find myself
Wishing that I had a dad like Jack
But it's just a tv show reflecting
The best and most flawed parts of a man
Who gave as much as he could of himself for his family

But here I sit at 12:07 A.M.
When I should be fast asleep
And I'm thinking about everything my own dad
Gave up for me - and of all of the many things he has done for me

I was born in New York and lived in Ohio for a short time
Before work brought my father to Pennsylvania
I was just old enough to begin pre-school
Now I'm not entirely sure when
For I didn't learn until I was much older
But at one point in time
My father was offered a job in West Virginia
This would have meant a higher salary
And being closer to the rest of his family:
My half siblings, his parents, and his sisters
Yet for some reason - he chose my chance at stability
I had made friends and even at such a young age

When I could have assimilated well to a new environment
He didn't want to uproot me and disrupt my life

And now I keep thinking about all of the little things
That I have overlooked or taken for granted my whole life
Like how he would come home from a long day at work
And sit on the living room floor with me
Playing with Barbie dolls, My Little Pony
Or my personal favorite: Teenage Mutant Ninja Turtle action figures

He always let me be the banker when we played Monopoly
Even though I had absolutely no concept of money
I just liked the pretty pastel colors of the paper
Around Christmastime, I always seemed to get the flu
So many of my childhood years I spent sick on the couch
And I would miss out getting to sit on Santa's lap, telling him what I
wanted for Christmas
But I could always count on a knock at the door before the holiday arrived
And standing on the other side would be Santa and Mrs. Clause
With a sack full of gifts for a sick little girl

I *knew* that I was special - because even when I was sick - Santa never
forgot me
And I was - special that is - because my dad never forgot me
I don't know how, but my dad knew the man who dressed up as Santa
every year
So my parents would leave a bag of gifts out on the porch for when Santa
arrived
And it made me believe in more magic than most kids could ever ask for
If that isn't something straight out of the Jack Pearson playbook

Then I don't know what is

Actually no -
That is a out of my dad's very own playbook
Because he came along in my life before "This Is Us" ever premiered
Most people have probably stopped reading by now
But I'm not writing this for "most people"
This is for my dad

On holidays such as Valentine's Day when he was out of town for work
I could always expect flowers or some type of gift to be delivered to me
At the time, I resented these meaningful gestures
Because it was just a reminder that my dad wasn't around as much as I
would have liked
But when he and my mom divorced, he traveled a lot for work
Because he was doing the very best that he could
And working his ass off to provide me with a comfortable life

When I was a bratty, ungrateful teenage girl
My dad would get me every other weekend
I would have a sleepover with my best friends
And my dad would always come in
With pizza, pop, and a plethora of other snacks
He never complained about having a houseful of teenage girls
(Except the one night we put peanut butter in Leah's hair -
                    we were giggling so much that it woke him up)

He would drive my friends and me forty minutes to the movies and mall
He drove us to the sketchy Lake Dances on Friday nights which was a half
an hour away

Listen to a bunch of giddy, boy-crazed girls the whole way there
And then drive the half an hour back to pick us up a few hours later
Only to listen to us giggle and gossip about our time at the dance
We were in our own world, and I completely ignored him on those rides
But never once did my dad complain about any of this

At sixteen I wanted to see an actor from a soap opera my friends and I
watched
So for my birthday, my dad drove my best friend, sister, and me to
Toronto
Just to see this actor speak on stage and hopefully get to go up and meet
him in person
(Yes - I actually did get to go up on stage, hug him, and I have my picture
taken with him)

In college, I wanted to meet Nicholas Sparks when he was speaking in
Philadelphia
My dad was on vacation at the time with my stepmom and my sister
But he agreed to come and pick me up when I lived outside of Pittsburgh
And go out of his way to take me to Philadelphia all because I wanted to
be a writer
(Yes - I also got to hug Nicholas Sparks and have my picture taken with
him)

My dad is an incredible man
He helped me out financially while I was
In college
After college
Working my first job in my career field
Getting my Master's Degree

Moving to another state

He
Paid off the last part of my Master's Degree
And helped me out when I was short on rent
Or needed extra money for groceries
Paid for part of my trip to Europe because I had to reschedule due to a
funeral
And the list could go on for miles

I owe my dad (and stepmom) a good amount of money (and gratitude)
And I slowly try to chip away at the debt I will never be able to fully repay
But it doesn't matter what I do or how hard I try
I will never be able to repay my dad back
Monetarily or with the same zeal of gratitude and love
That he has shown me my entire life
I will never be able to thank him enough
Even if I spent every second of every day saying the words

So yeah - maybe my dad isn't some Jack Pearson fictional character
But I have one hell of a dad who is real and even better

-LiAnnah Jameson-

Memories / Daddy's Little Girl

Strong hands / soft voice
Fish fry at the river / boiled peanuts / porch swing
John Deere / Johnny Cash
Spaghetti westerns / race cars / wrestling superheroes
Swimmin' in the creek / playing in the sprinkler
Pickin' pecans / choir practice
Front yard baseball / long haul trucker
Dusty dirt roads / fields of cotton
Summer sunsets / hazel eyes smiling at mine
Bedtime stories / waking up to waffles & bacon

-Sarah Herrin-

Funny Things

Funny things that make me think of dad:
brown buttons, windshield wipers and elevator doors. Books with dust
jackets
braving this cold world. Oh, and gas station coffee, no smoking signs.
Even the way markers draw ink lines.

-Heini Talip-

<u>Safe</u>

you're like me
not like me
sometimes
but I like you
all the time
in dusty evenings
and late night
leavings
and home cooked
meals on
plates that don't match
and laughter we catch
about trees we've climbed
in winter
always fallen into those
steady hands
of yours
without a bruise or
scratch

-Maya Elphick-

Last of a Dying Breed

a quiet enigma
full of rather underestimated charisma;
an old school cat, man –
such a splendid simplicity
that would drive most insane.

not much into fashion
not much into fakers,
just a powerful passion
for living strong
through the pain.

just grab 'em a drink
grab 'em some good company,
and a slow-movin' clock –

cause my daddy, he ain't perfect,
but you damn well bet,
you'll remember his name.

-Kevin Vargo-

Sanctuary

My squinted eyes scan over faded photographs
of a timeless wedding which resembled a greek gods palace
the beings inside— my parents who always continue to radiate light
with my dad alike Ra calling upon the dawn
only allowing the moon to cast a shadow over their undying love
flowing within them to never let time hinder its strength unlike
the wrinkles in pale beside melanin skin and frail bones
differing the passion that drove them home after work
when all hope is lost and they only had touch to keep them sane
still I see my fathers coarse hands rub circles on my mother's olive skin
her solace— a cure for all stresses and anxieties which clouded his brain
calming him once again to be at peace and furthering his loving gaze
we all are gifted with when food is served or hugs are offered warm
alongside a comforting piece of advice i'll cherish with all my heart
while my parents found a way to make themselves fall more in love
they wouldn't of been able to without my fathers stable mind
with his ability to lessen sadness and other negative thoughts
he is our sanctuary in a sky with clouds.

-Lara Decastecker-

English Weather

You never heard the rain
until morning came
and the sun had dried up
all the puddles.
Halos of light kissing trees
and frost coating leaves
that glisten against that cool breeze.
So we sat on the wall
watching new rain fall
and counted the puddles together,
because you made me see
the undeniable beauty of
real English weather.

-Maya Elphick-

- Becoming -

Becoming You

As a boy you were taught in only blacks and whites
Sharp edges with precise lines
Love, yes, but distilled and bland
Laws and standards in full measure
But now, 40 years later, that boy is a dad
And your daughters have reshaped you
With sparkles and tap shoes and giggles
Grace poured out and faith twirling in tulle
Fatherhood rests easy on you

-Lacie Wright-

Lessons

He was broken
And we showed him
How to be
Free
And innocent
How to love
Unconditionally
And then he did

- Lesley Worthington-

Rough Childhood

i did it,
my first varsity score!
i can remember
the smell of the grass
i can remember
the feel of the heat.
i can remember
looking up
at mom
jumping out of her seat,
and then over
at you,
gleaming with pride,
almost stuck in disbelief.

you'd engrained it in your head,
that there was simply no way
i could have been yours
when at my age,

for you,
things were a little different
if you didn't do your chores,
and those dreams of playin' ball
had long since been dead.

after all,
how could sports be a thing
with so many walls to fix
from your body being thrown
and so many walls to tear down
from sleepless nights left all alone?
a present father,
but his absence weighed heavy,
how could you catch a touchdown
when at 13,
you were forced
to be grown?

-Kevin Vargo-

Synonym of Sacrifice

Once upon a time there lived a noble man,
Who was asked by God to sacrifice his dear son,
Even though it was his test and a blessing in disguise,
Determined to serve his Lord, he did abide with heavy hearted cries.

That one moment is marked in history,
Only to remind us of the greatness of his story.

Many such figures have time and again been tested,
Yet no one really understands that it's unwillingly they stay restricted.

For all of us have been guided by them in our lives,
Always we question their stands and resistance,
Thoroughly you may feel bitter at times of his dominance,
Had it not been for that benevolent significance,
Each one of us would not have tackled troubles with resilience.
Remember Zan!! Fathers are true synonyms to sacrifice.

-Zan-

The Sower

I held them,
my only care,
two dreams,
from seeds,

nothing more important,
than dreams,
dreams,
and water,
and time,
and in time,

it was they,
holding mine,
like crystals, clear,
two lights, less near,

life giving, taking away,
no one there, to say,
no one here, to say,
to sow,
so they,

not knowing,
seeds growing,
in a distance,
the sowing,
of a father.

And a good one.

-J. Savarese-

My Dad

My dad has been through a lot
He was beaten like pots
And Pans
However he took a stand
To stop the cycle
Of the mistakes
Of which held him as the stake
Of abuse

-Will Berry-

Lessons

You Gave Life

While our culture teetered on its indecision between female infanticide and the glorification of the Hindu goddess,

you my father rose like air above the breath of bullets and bouquets.

You gave life, if not birth, to bridges and balconies for my paper heart to take a leap of faith from;

to imbibe without a doubt than I am indeed an equal.

Sometimes falling off the ledge of entropic certainty to sleep between the snowdrops

and other times to be reincarnated as a hibakusha wildflower warrior.

You coursed through my veins hand in hand with mother, an ocean swell of intrepid dragon hearts and sun drenched dandelion fuzz,

so I knew to conquer the world with both the nurturing aurora of love and the corrective crack of lightning.

-Ambica Gossain-

Sunnies

Sunflowers are the light of my universe. I don't know when sunflowers became my definitive favorite, but the entire family knows it.

They are big, bright, bold, and beautiful. I would have probably used those words to describe me before the break up, that is. I was super loud and cheerful. I was a theatre kid on steroids – everything had to be over the top and dramatic.

You knew my relationship had been a pretty toxic one, and it left me a shell of the person I once was. I wasn't so big, so loud, so bright anymore. I knew you could sense the difference in me, but you didn't know exactly how to help. You don't really dwell on emotional things. They usually develop into some sort of joke to ease the blow of whatever bad news is to come. But I think you knew this was bigger than any joke.

It was my first year in four years being single on Valentine's Day. I came home from college that weekend, all the way to Greenville, because I couldn't bear being surrounded by kids in love. I even made a hair appointment – I was ready for some change - or maybe I was just pretending to get by.

"What are you going to do to your head?" you asked me before I left the house.

"Something. I don't know."

I couldn't stop thinking about how alone I was – I guess wallowing in self pity was my thing for awhile.

Self pity also made me chop my hair off to my shoulders. Take that, sadness! My stylist curled it all nice, and, for a moment, I felt like a rockstar. I ran to the car, fumbling with the keys.

Sunflowers were sitting on my driver's seat. At first, I was slightly alarmed. How did they get there...? Did I leave my car unlocked the entire time I was getting my hair done? How could I possibly have a secret admirer?

Turns out I did.

I opened the car door and just held them in my hands for a moment. Sunnies' stems are like big, bulky green stalks, and they felt sturdy in my hands. The yellow heads nodded as if I needed a reminder. A reminder that I was so loved. A reminder that I could be loud and big and bold and beautiful again. That I was enough.

A reminder that you would always be my very first (and best) Valentine.

Thanks for the sunny love, Dad.

-Eloise-

A Father's Love

You taught me it was possible
For a man to love me tirelessly, endlessly and unconditionally
Without my inevitable heartbreak

-M.R.S.-

Dad, Hero

There was always an extra quarter
For the gumball machine
You drew stick figure chickens
Played hide and seek with Bunny
Told bedtime ghost trucker stories
And how three brothers stood up
One by one on the school bus
To protect the fourth youngest
In the garden you gave
Johnny Cash wisdom
People stare because
They wish they had your bravery
You're stubborn when hurt
And still won't travel - yet
You raised me, quiet but strong
How to stand on my own
You taught me, never cry wolf
Stick up for the underdog
Look after the outcast
Work hard, tell the truth
And always, speak out.

-Sarah Herrin-

My Dear

There are a few people in your life you meet
and who are special to you.
You argue with these very ones
when you're younger.
That makes you grow and gives you strength.
You test your limits.
But simply for the reason that you yearn for
freedom and at the same time look
for a feeling of home and belonging.
And later they offer you many possibilities
without interfering in your life.
Yes, I had it good. I was lucky.
I could always be and become
what I wanted to be.
And yet you meet people on your way
who want to tell you what you can and can't do.
Because they need you in a certain way.
I took a long time until I recognized this and
believed them for some years.
Or maybe they don't imagine life any other way.
They are just different and their own projection
meets you.
Glad that I met you. And you taught me differently.
I should have remembered that. Luckily I did, finally.

-Miriam Otto-

College

as a parting sentiment,
she hugged me
and he

shook my hand.

and at that moment,
it was then i knew
that i'd grown

from a boy to a man.

-Kevin Vargo-

My Blood

It's not always been easy,
I'll be the first to admit
that you've hurt,
she's hurt
and I've hurt.
But can't you see it's bound us
for blood is thicker than water
and our rivers gush with it.
We've dangled our legs
and thrown a line,
pushed each other in,
made swings from ties
and laughed about the times
we've left behind
but will never
ever forget.

-Maya Elphick-

A Journey With My Father

My dearest Dad,

It is now two months since we arrived home from our greatly anticipated travels together and I have been intending for some time now, to write to you about the trip and to share my thoughts and feelings with you. It has been a revelatory process to reflect on our journey and realise just how different the experiences now seem when viewed through the lens of hindsight.

The trip was undoubtedly a 'once-in-a-lifetime' experience that provided an opportunity neither of us had entertained before: travelling together as father and daughter, and at the ages of 82 and 59! The challenges were many, particularly as both of us have become used to living alone, and the thought of having to accommodate each other's eccentricities twenty-four hours a day for six weeks was not the least of them!

I think we managed remarkably well despite the anticipated and unanticipated challenges.

I'm sure each of us has constructed our shared experiences differently with regard to significance and meaning. For you, the trip was an opportunity to return to places you had visited with Mum as both a pilgrim and a tourist. You selected places with purpose, knowledge and a strong sense of personal and religious history. I realised early on, that although I didn't share this focus with you, the opportunity to accompany you was a special opportunity that may never avail itself again. This aspect was more significant to me than the actual travelling; as I knew that if I were planning a trip overseas it would be to different destinations with quite different emphases.

Our first week in Athens was delightful and enabled us to gently settle in to each other, greatly needed after having lived in different States for close to thirty years. It was relaxing and enjoyable and I was grateful for the opportunity to also have the time and space to discuss the issues that arose for me. It was challenging at times to be confronted by some of the feelings that were surfacing from my childhood, triggered by what I perceived as your controlling patterns. But it was healing to discuss this openly with you and I was heartened by your willingness to personally accommodate the issues we discussed.

Once you became ill in Istanbul, the subsequent two weeks of travel through Croatia, Bosnia Herzegovina, Italy and Ireland were coloured very differently. The focus for me suddenly shifted to restoring your failing health, and ultimately, without sounding too dramatic, keeping you alive. The isolation I felt throughout this time, amidst my fears for your wellbeing, was very stressful and it was such a relief to see you gradually recover once discharged from Dublin's Accident and Emergency. I coped by consciously focusing on present time, which helped quell the rising feelings of disappointment and sadness that could have dominated my emotions in the realization that the trip, and your health, appeared to be disintegrating before us.

It was wonderfully restorative for you to have those two weeks of being driven around Ireland, although it remained considerably stressful for me bearing all the travel and accommodation responsibility, along with niggling uncertainties about the state of your health. But overall, Ireland was a truly wonderful aspect of our trip.

Once you were home safely and seemed to make a good recovery from the pneumonia that ailed you for four of the six weeks, our travels, on reflection, began to take on a different hue. I realized that more than anything else, the trip for me had evolved into a journey of emotional growth with you, my father. I also realized that I had not seen you sick or dependent on anyone, until then. Much of the time, the persona you present to the world is of a strong, confident, capable, gregarious and sociable person. At times I found this irritating as I felt these characteristics often established barriers and masked your authentic emotions. However, during your illness I witnessed aspects of you that I had seldom, if ever, seen before.

Significantly, you had to relinquish control and trust me to manage everything. You were also very vulnerable, both physically and emotionally, and this created an intimacy I had not experienced with you previously. There were such beautifully tender moments when I was caring for you, feeding you, showering you and just being with you that expanded my love for you in ways that I would not perhaps have experienced had you not become ill. It was incredibly touching to see how emotional you became at times and how loving and tender you could be in your frailty. I enjoyed your sense of humour and listening to the numerable recollections of life experiences that surfaced during the many hours spent by your bedside and while driving around the country of our ancestors.

The laughs we shared about being mistaken for husband and wife, your medication rituals, dentures, noisy breathing whilst asleep and the constant misplacement or loss of your belongings were also enriching and incredibly memorable. We shared some very, very special times together Dad. With all of my heart, I want to thank you for your love, compassion, generosity and the opportunity you gave me to develop a greater understanding of who you are, both as a man and my father. Our journey together was a wonderful gift that has greatly enriched me, and I will cherish it and you, always.

Your ever-loving and grateful daughter,
-Kathleen-

Universes

You are not perfect
but neither is the sun nor the moon,
orbs of life we find so much
comfort in.
Every shooting star
I have seen
has faded with the wish or dream
I have pinned upon its light,
but you have stayed
in clear sight
my moon in a jar
my constant star.
Like the sun rising in the east,
I can predict the motions of your brain
like no one else's,
a metronome heart if ever I heard one.
The ticks keep me sane.
A rhythm that eases the uneven shaking
of quaking thoughts and breaking bodies.
I can rely on the stars in your eyes
unlike those above my head,
as they do not shine for me
nor any other.

So when our rare nights of quiet contentment
come around,
I do not need to look up
to see the galaxy around me
as I can depend upon
the universe we have created.

-Maya Elphick-

Classic Rock 'n' Roll

takin' it easy
with the eagles
or havin' a spirit in the sky
with norman –
back in black
with angus
or a red barchetta
with geddy
hangin on 10th ave.,
freezin' out with bruce and the big man
or on cloud nine
with the temptations
even riding through a storm
with mr. mojo risin',
or a landslide of dreams
with lindsey and stevie,

no matter what it is
or where it is
or who it's with –
you taught me
music is the only thing
That can make it all make sense.
and for that
i thank you, dad.

-Kevin Vargo-

My Father Like a Pink Rose

My father like a pink rose:
Common, distant, full of thorns.

My father like a rising tide:
Eroding, thoughtless, could drown inside.

My father like an autumn breeze:
He pollinate the rotten trees.

My father like an evening fire:
He singe, he burn, he crackle with ire.

My father like a household pet:
He bark, he shriek, then shit instead.

My father a hyena, a cruel beast:
Deprived of love, a carcass his feast.

Yet still my father like the night:
Inside his madness found dots of light.

He teach what not to be,
And this I celebrate.

He teach that life
Mean I shape my fate.

I learn my life like
A birthday cake,

Every moment sweet:
Nothing cruelty can take away.

So father's day I say myself,
You beautiful nature
                          You beautiful sound.

My experience I celebrate.
My father's lessons

Necessary – and profound.

-Robert Malka-

No Value

Strange how lessons are learnt
Sometimes so easy, so smooth
At others, through sorrows
Through the pain of doubtful tomorrows
Which no balm can soothe

I learnt this by the bedside
Of one I loved with high esteem
He was our family provider
A father defending us from any outsider
A natural leader of his small team

Touched by the cursed caress of cancer
That most tyrant of diseases
That cuts through every dream
That cuts through hope to the extreme
And will be with us till Hell freezes

For six long, short years and then a half
I was his escort, nurse and friend
Hopes rose and hopes fell
Radio & chemo staving off Death's knell
At Marsden we saw others meet their dismal end

I left my business far behind
Though in trusted hands, for sure
I saw my own vanities, pictorial
Gold trinkets and clothes, sartorial
I took off those symbols of a pride impure

After all this ignominious time
Of disappointment and nightmare pains
Of surgery, drugs and passionate prayer
Of doctors, treatments, shattered hopes and despair
He left us on a Sunday morn, freed from Life's chains

'Twas then I realised the truth
That escapes us all in this world so crude
Love is free... or not at all
Faith too deep to find in any shopping mall
A kiss or genuine human warmth can't be accrued

It comes for zero cost
It comes from soul to soul, from genuine friend
For whatever you possess.....
Whatever you can buy and sell
Once finally you assess this hell
Has no value in the end

-David Bentata-

Epitaphs

Prioritizing priorities,
You showed family was the top of your list.

Work hard, play hard
That devil-may-care attitude was hard to resist.

I know, because I inherited that trait -
Set all else aside,
For time, with family it can all wait.

Who knew how important this lesson would be?
But when we lost mom, I found my heart to be guilt free.

You taught me well, where the important stuff lies-
It can be found in no bank,
But locked only inside.

For not one man wishes they had worked more
-You are found to remind-
When the Lord calls home
And it is time for their own 'goodbye'.

-Austie M. Baird-

Our Garden

spring is here
and the roses have sprung
and the tulips we planted
many moons ago,
again, they've bloomed
and under the porch light they glow.
our garden, our garden
sacred as can be
as a kid, a whole new
secret world for me.
as a man though,
tormented by thorns
jabbed in your side
one after another
from a childhood gone awry,
our garden, our garden
sacred as can be
just a simple place
- I see it now -
where you went to feel free.

-Kevin Vargo-

My Guru

It was my father's formidable stature, prostrated in prayer, that taught me humility comes in all shapes and sizes. At five years old, I used to seize every opportunity to clamber onto his tiger back, my pretend sword in hand, to assume the role of the avenging goddess Ambica, my father had named me after. Each visit to the temple culminated with him touching my feet to accrue blessings, he assured me all little Hindu girls had been enchanted as incarnations of divinity itself; which he then brushed over his eyelids, to transfer the energy of the spiritual universe to his soul.

He repeated this ritual everyday before we sat down to breakfast, following his narration of how he and grandmother had confounded the gods with their respective wishes for a girl child and boy progeny and I'd giggle, because clearly he'd triumphed. Grandmother's futile attempt at masking her disappointment was always evident as she bellowed that the (Kaliyuga) fourth and final stage of the world had arrived, signifying moral decay and hence the end of the world. We should have been mortified, but my grandmother had spoiled us rotten, so we knew her heart was in the right place. A lack of education coupled with generations of conditioning had just left her no alternative but to question the very existence of being a girl, albeit having been one herself a very long time ago. But your heart doesn't always listen to what your mind's been told and hers was no different.

My father showed me by his example, everyday of my life, that the faithful practice of religion meant identifying the inherent goodness we are each born with, irrespective of cast, creed, gender, nationality, skin colour or sexuality, among other distinguishing characteristics that make us human. He taught me that if we just dig deep enough, we eventually strike gold and then all we need is the warmth of love, to melt and return us to the original moulds god had intended for us.

-Ambica Gossain-

The Simplest Treasure

He's quiet, unassuming
but still, commanded respect.
No need for false façade
he lived his life direct.
For no masks were needed
a simple life sustained.
Truth was unimpeded
his family, the gold he claimed.

The lessons that I learned
the memories of my Dad,
were kindness above all
and to be Humanity's Comrade.
For he led by example,
the light shining though his eyes.
He modelled something that
couldn't be taught - how to empathize.

Although now he's gone
a legacy gift was blessed.
His treasured kids and grandkids
to live on with Life's Precious Zest.

-Linda Lokhee-

Family Trait

My father has a particular passion for the natural world.

I suppose you could say it was a family trait passed down to him from his mother, who learned it from her father, who was, after all, one of the very first forest rangers.

My father did his family duty and I cannot remember a time in my life when we did not spend a significant amount of time revering in the beauty of "God's church" as my father often referred to the out-of-doors.

Having small children never seem to burden my dad, he simply packed us along – young girls can easily mimic the bugle of an elk in rut, and small boys make great fishermen as they grow up!

He taught us the basics: how to build a fire, that water runs downhill, the sun rises in the east and sets in the west, and to always pack out your trash- for only the wild should remain to be another man's treasure.

And then he taught us more: how to spot signs of wildlife, how do identify the conifer trees, where to locate the dippers and Cassiopeia, and which mushrooms were the right mushrooms to eat.

Our nature exploring ran far and deep - admiring the beauty of God's country became an intricate part of me.

It is something special to be able to hand down, this family knowledge of the land taught to me by my dad. Now my own kids take part in the fun, as we work to teach them about the wide world that thrives off the sun.

-Austie M. Baird-

Wishes

Father

For every person who tells me I have your face
I hope,
one day,
they will see
I wear your heart too.

-L.T.Pelle-

A Father's Hope

"Dad? I asked as he pulled the car into the garage.
It was late evening and just the two of us - a rare occasion.

"Do you think," I continued, "that I will ever meet a man
who is half as wonderful as you?"

"I hope one day," he began, "you meet a man who is even better than me."

I found the idea of that hard to fathom
And I have yet to find that man for myself
But I'm not ready to give up hope yet.

-LiAnnah Jameson-

Dad's Stamp

I have never really been one
to mind what others think
but I wonder if you see me
in constant pursuit of your approval
-M.R.S.-

New Shirt

watching you
wring out your sleeves,
and rid yourself
from the sweat of stress
and the blood of burden -
my, oh my, what a sight.
we even got you a new shirt
so you can rest peacefully!
i just wish so badly
i could see you (again)
wear this one out.

-Kevin Vargo-

I Did It My Way

You told me we would meet in Grand Central Station. By now, I almost had the 6 train memorized - 96th, 86th, 77th, 68th, 59th, 51st, Grand Central 42nd Street. The air was just beginning to bite. North Carolina doesn't even pinch; it eventually gets colder, but the heave of humidity was always lurking under. It was raining the day you came, so I grabbed my red coat with the deep pockets. I should have put on my rain boots to match, but I forgot in my hurried skip to the train. I saw you a month ago, the day you moved me in, but it was exciting. We never had just us time.

Standing by the big clock in the center of the station, you had your black duffel slung haphazardly across your shoulder, your eyes fixated on your IPhone, glasses hanging on the edge of your nose. I wondered if you always wore your glasses now. I wonder what else I was missing, moving so far away. I awkwardly run up to you, your arms squeezing me a little too hard like they do. You always hold a second longer than I think you will.

"Let's get a drink," you suggest, pointing to the bar.

I agree, even though you know I don't like alcohol very much. I forget what to order that sounds appetizing, and you order me a vodka cranberry. It's too strong, but I don't say anything. Sitting here, I can see now that there is more salt than pepper in your hair.

It couldn't have happened all at once. The blackish-brown will all be gone soon. That realization makes me sadder than it should. I didn't know you then, but we have pictures of a lanky kid with black hair in bright neon shorts, your mouth wide open with the biggest grin. I wonder if I would have liked you as a teenager - a young adult. Were you now just more adult-ier? When do you advance from young adult to adult? Does the salt just show your age on the outside? What happens if you don't want to grow up?

"How is work?" I ask, knowing you hate it.

"It's work."

You take the last sip of your rum and coke for good measure. I force myself to drink the rest of mine, the hint of cranberry as my own relief.

"Have you been to the New York Public Library?" you ask me.

"No. Why?"

"The lion. We have to go see the lions. It's on your list," you smile.

You remember my New York list that I made at the age of fourteen. I started reading at the age of four, holding the book upside down, but by god did I memorize every word. I loved to read ever since, just right side up this time. It was even more magical that way. I wanted to move to New York City after I starred as Charlotte in Charlotte's Web in our community theater. Imagine a black leotard that covered my entire body but my face...and feather boas for arms. Who knew I would get stage fright and the biggest adrenaline rush of my life all at the same time? I may have been a spider, but I was hooked.

I knew I was going to make it big someday. I made a list of everything I would do and see; I absolutely had to sit on the public library's steps in between the two big lion statues. They guarded the most famous steps...to me anyway. Fast forward to graduate school me with a B.A. in English and in NYC for an entirely different reason...but I made it, right? I almost felt embarrassed.

"Oh, no, it's okay. It's raining outside," I said.

"So what? Let's go! It's around the corner."

You leave cash at the bar and begin walking away from me. I follow complacently. I forget these streets are your old stomping grounds. Brooklyn born and raised, an eighteen year old straight out of high school into work in the Big Apple. You are walking as if you have a thirty year old map engraved in your head, no hesitations. I wonder if I will ever be that good at direction - be that good at anything. You are jumping puddles in front of taxis, power walking with your hands in your jean pockets. Who was this person? It was if I had a glimpse of younger you - Robert. It's the oddest sensation, like the age when one suddenly realizes his/her parents have a real name. Maybe I was at that age when you realize your parent is a person. A person just like me.

The rain drops have blurred my glasses, but I give two thumbs up for the picture you take of me, shivering.

"One more stop!"

Another? We back track quickly. I am gritting my teeth and I cannot see enough to cross the street. It was as if you were invincible to the rain, the cold, the blurred glasses. We stop at 485 Lexington Avenue.

"Take a picture of me and send it to Mom. We met at this building 27 years ago."

Your eyes peer up at the building. You pat the numbers tenderly, recalling something you wouldn't say.

"Do you miss it? Here?"

There is a long pause, baby wrinkles beginning to crease the edge of your lips.

"The South is much...slower than here. I think maybe it has ruined me."

I want to tell you I don't agree, but I say nothing. I snap the picture, your face painted with that goofy grin like the younger pictures, your mouth hanging open. The same person...just with salt and pepper hair as your award for getting through.

"Are you happy now?" I ask.

I don't realize my double meaning at the time.

"I did it my way," you sing.

You always make jokes out of serious things. It's Frank Sinatra. You always tell me this when I am down; you also constantly remind me that it has to be played at your funeral. I hope it's true.

-Eloise-

The Distance Between Us

I have always thought of my father and I
As having an imaginary thread between us
That links our lives together
And so when one of us dies
The other one will, too
Because I know that I can't imagine
Living a single day without my father
And that thread is the only thing
That connects us together

My mother and I
Are (almost) exactly alike
At least that is what my father has always said
It was the reason for so much discord
In the house I lived in with my mother

My mother is emotional -
Tumultuous, determined, unpredictable, loquacious
My father is logical -
Stubborn, quiet, reserved, old-fashioned

I know my father loves me
To the deepest core of his heart and soul
He has been the most supportive, generous, and kindest
Man that I have ever known
I am lucky - I am blessed
To be able to call him my father

But sometimes I wish
There wasn't such an emotional disconnect between us

I feel like we are on two remote islands
With an entire ocean separating us
A distance we cannot breach
No ship or boat to even meet in the middle

I do have a small dingy with a leak
And two wooden oars that tire out my arms
From trying so hard to row to him
Needless to say I don't get very far
Before the water begins to fill up my dingy
And I have to give up and turn around before I sink

Meanwhile my father stays on his island
I wave to him
Sometimes he waves back
I call out his name
Until my voice is hoarse and starts to crack
But he can't seem to hear my cries
And I'm only met
With his silence in my solitude

- LiAnnah Jameson-

Chest

I still have that picture,
moment sealed in sepia hue,
what was the beginning of me,
and the beginning of you.

I lay on your chest sleeping,
wrinkly in my newborn pain
and you look tired, so tired,
hair sticking every which way.

I was a crying infant - colic they said.
Soothe her, hold her,
it will go away.

I'm sure
you were a mess, more like a puddle than a chest
but you were just starting,
and so was I.

For that ribcage you laid me on
was really a stage, a soil so I could bloom,
a diving board to jump from,
as I did, for sure.

I wish I could remember
the calm that chest created,
for my crying days are still not over,
no doubt they never will.

-Heini Talip-

Depression

dear dad,
i wish i could've got the chance
to tell you in person
how sorry i am
for always mistaking
your mental illness
for you just 'not getting it'
or because i thought you were 'mean.'
you were anything but mean –
you were a broken man
with the biggest of hearts,
too far gone
before you even got here,
and with too big a heart
not to die young
like the rest of the legends.

-Kevin Vargo-

Thank You

Dad's Identity

Sometimes it slips my mind
That you are just a person
Not a superhero, nor a god
It's easy to confuse the three
But if every time I've needed saving, you've rescued me
And every time I've prayed for clarity, you've guided me
Maybe, you're more than human afterall

-M.R.S.-

Poet's Paternity

I know where my melancholy comes from.
I know the birth place of my pitiful screams.
I know the origin of my downward posture, the reason
I love the colour blue.

Thank you for my poetic vocal cords,
thank you for my flowering soul.

-Heini Talip-

Dream Chaser

In almost every way
A southern gentleman, my Dad
(And all that that entails)
This man of science and of faith
Of loyalty and trust
By value of his work was known
His wisdom and his grace

Now several years beyond his death
I have become my father, some
(And all that that entails!)
It thus might come as a surprise
His greatest of all gifts to me
The gift this man of science
And of faith and law and work
Was nurtured in the gardens of
His father and his aunt
Was nurtured as he grew up in
The grandeur of Pike's Peak
Was captured in his endless quest
Of oil beneath the soil
Of bayous, farms, and desert and
Concealed below the Gulf
Was nurtured in the future
represented by his boys
Was nurtured by the constancy
Of his beloved Billie Jo

And only now I see with eyes
Now older than his ever were
The gift he gave was his blessing
To seek the dreams that we would choose
Wherever they may come or go
With chosen ones who share our chase
So thank you, Dad, for I am blessed
A dream chaser I did become

-Russell Willis

Becoming a man

I knew you when your face was smooth and your hands were soft
Your heart was open: untested and wild
Now you're weathered and battered
You've seen war
And the desert sands have worn down your bright edges.
The boy who once left is now a man who stays.

-Lacie Wright-

A Persevering Father

Dad,
There could not be a greater father in all the world
Than the one God gifted this little girl.
With steady hands and a selfless heart
You helped me grow
Flourishing in all you've taught,
No matter the struggles
Or the triumphs I walk.
You provided
No matter your hardships
Or clumsy mistakes
Despite the expectations of everyone around you
And the stigma of a single Dad
I am who I am today
Because of you
Humble yet proud Is how I hold my head.
And now I will give such steady hands to the rest of the world
As you have exemplified
Through a father's mighty persevering faith
I am who I am today.

-Crystal Nicole-

The Day Dad Turned 45

It was your birthday
The gift?
My broken heart
You didn't flinch at the news
Didn't raise a single question
You simply revved up your truck
And drove hundreds of miles
To help me pick up the pieces
Salvage what was left
On our return home
Mumford sang
Where you invest your love
You invest your life
And I was so grateful
To be your passenger
And to leave him behind

-M.R.S.-

Diary Entries

Dear Father,

Five years ago, we were happy as if we had a makeshift fountain of youth.
We played piano for hours as I smiled in silence while we created our melodies.
Even though you were anxious and always had to take a certain pill before concerts;
you still played and thus, I didn't mind.
You held me in your arms when I was sad.
You were my idol and everything I dreamt to be.

Two years ago, I felt lost and I was exasperated.
I quit piano.
I locked myself in my room and screamed when you entered.
I poured my heart into my studies and my mind into fantasy books.
I wanted to run away from my reality.
I'm sorry I said I didn't love you.

A year ago, I told you I had to grow up.
I have to learn to drive.
I have to go to college soon.
I cried myself to sleep.
I cried because I still felt like a child.
A part of me still wanted to be your child.

Now, you're my source of strength.
I'm learning how to drive thanks to you.
You overcame your anxiety and decided to teach me how to drive.

I am content in the space I find myself in
I feel unconditionally safe and loved.
Just as importantly, I hope you do too.

Truly, your daughter.

P.s. I love you.

-Lara Decastecker-

Thanks, Dad

Things fathers pass to their daughters:
weird knees,
the sharp edges of a rose,
and sometimes
those hobbit hairs
on your big toes.

-Heini Talip-

Learning to Measure

I tried to write a poem for you
But it wouldn't come out right.

How do you put that kind of 'thanks' into words,
For the man who gave you life?

The one who picked your mother,
Bought your childhood home,
Taught you how to love others,
And how to tell you're grown?

There are simply not words
To give proper thanks,
To the first man to love me
Through all of my mistakes.

To the one who was my first best friend
-My rescuer and guardian-
No matter how many lines I write,
Or how carefully I choose these rhymes,
No poem will do justice to you
Dear dad, daddy, oh father of mine.

Thank you for all you've given,
All you are,
All you've been.
Thank you for being my measure
Of the worth of all other men.

-Austie M. Baird-

Daddy-O

The hero of my story has always been you,
an audience member in a crowded theater
with a bouquet of flowers -
a standing ovation on your heart;
an outdoorsman leading your ducklings
on bicycles traveling down a mountain,
creek water in your hair; a coffee partner
sipping life's questions with caramel.
Your love is the greatest gift,
your support the greatest answer.

-Eloise-

Our Patriarch

Grey hair on his head shows
he's a man of age. Wrinkles
upon his face bare witness
to the fact he's a thinker.
Paitence in his dark eyes
reflect that this man is a
wise sage. Scars upon his
rugged hands prove he is a
hard worker. His sun worn
skin reads like a map of his
years trekking many
mileage. Patches throughout
his garment reveal him as a
man of service not someone
whose status is amongst the
"proper". Yet when his family
looks at him we see a man
whose our patriarch since
the dawn of another age.

-Steve Gonzales, Jr.-

There's Always a Piece of Heart for You

I'm sorry for the tone of voice I took at times
When frustration left me poor at communication,
Oh, how smart I became with rebuttals after puberty
But my argumentative nature was not reserved for you,
For you I reserved an entire ventricle of space for my love
Even when I didn't let the three syllables free,
I loved you.
I love you now, as I write these lines,
As I think about all the times you smiled just from looking at me
So many days spent walking sugar cane fields on afternoons off
And driving around to nowhere just to talk
You are still my first call when I have news to share
Comfort level with you only continues to rise
Though we may sometimes fight
You are first and most important man in my life.

-Abeer A. Zayyad-

Similarities

I am passionate
And opinionated
Kind but impatient
I am strong
And resilient
But there's a softness in my heart
I love harder than most
I cherish, I protect
I show up for those I love best
I am my father's daughter

-M.R.S.-

Cornerstone Parables

Mom may have taught us that wise men build houses on stone;

But you, Dad, were the corner stone to our foundations,
Aligning us to the straight and narrow of the mortal world.

You were the block from which we learned to build with success.

-Austie M. Baird-

To Protect and Serve

i can't tell you how many times
i've started a sentence
or lead a conversation with,

"as the son of a policeman..."

the most sincere testament
to my regard for my father
and his sacrifice -
to all the men and women in blue,
and their willingness
to protect
and serve.

-Kevin Vargo-

Goodbyes

Honorable Man (My Dad)

Others honor his laugh,
and the faces he'd make,
and how everything, to him, was a joke,
I honor the sunflower seeds,
watching wrestling on tv,
and giant plumes of cigarette smoke,
He went to work everyday,
He was upstanding and dedicated
to his wife and all of their kids,
I grew into an honorable women,
Because of all the honor of him,
I went on to lead an honorable life,
He gave my husband an honorable wife,
As my father, the honor was his,
But the honor was truly ours,
To have such an honorable dad,
Until we buried him,
An honorable man.

-Bettie Schade-

Life Heist

Dear Dad, I miss you.
Your gentle manner
Your kind eyes
and the way you were
a Good Man
This dedication has my heart's
love
and all the aches:

Alzheimer's the thief
Creeping
    slowly
       silently
without a sound
Claiming pieces of you
little by little

Falling away
from oneself
Falling away
from family
Falling away
from life
Fading
    incognito
       surreptitiously

It didn't ask to take you
It just stole you away
    Q u i e t l y

-Linda Lokhee-

You Are

You are in every Daddy holding his daughter's hand
You are in the snippet of Australian accent I hear in line at the bank
You are in every chocolate dipped Dairy Queen ice cream
You are in the cloud of cigarette smoke I linger through outside the movies
You are in every tennis match on TV
You are in the pizza with pepperoni, green peppers, and mushrooms
You are in every moment of compassion for those less fortunate
You are in the news article lamenting the state of public education
You are in every smoker's hacking cough
You are in the heat of the vindaloo curry
You are in every red Toyota Corolla
You are in the stretch of highway where you took your last breath
You are in every pair of cheap men's shoes
You are in the dates of your birthday, your wedding anniversary, your death
You are in every chess game
You are in the empty Heineken bottles waiting to be returned
You are in every short fuse and over reaction
You are in meandering Sunday afternoon drives
You are in every hospital and funeral home
You are in mustard yellow corduroy bell bottoms
You are in every Easter Egg hunt and Christmas decoration
You are in the choppy lake at your favourite University town
You are in the kindness and humanity of your eldest grandson
You are in the national pride beating through the heart and soul of your granddaughter
You are in the brilliant wit and intelligence of your other grandson
You are still here

-Lesley Worthington-

The Man, Immortal

Playful smiles
-With that little boy twinkle-
Linger in eyes
That long since have wrinkles.

As I age, so does he
Yet time stands still
In the mind of the man
Who forever sees me
As his first baby.

That smile you see today
Stretches through time
To the photographs
And memories
Of a little girl
Who never quite grew up
To be as larger-than-life as he.

Untarnished by life
He stands before me
The man who held
My hand is his
When monsters crept
From under sheets
Or cars threatened
When crossing streets.

This man is a giant
-Formidable and fierce-
Strong and steady
Love gifts immortality,
Everlasting,
Without signs of aging
For daddy, from children.

-Austie M. Baird-

-Competition Winners-

Steady Hands: Odes to Our Fathers was born in a large part out of a writing competition held by A.B.Baird Publishing - these are the winners of that competition.

Grand Prize:
> Day of Rest- L.T. Pelle
> > (l.t.pelle)

First Runner Up:
> The Simplest Treasure- Linda Lokhee
> > (lindalokheeauthor)

People's Choice:
> The Midnight Train- Ambica Gossain
> > (tryst_with_fiction)

We wish to give a sincere 'thank you' to all who participated in this writing competition or voted in the people's choice, you all rock!

-Index-

A listing of each author found in this anthology and which pages you can find their work.

Dear Readers,

As always, we at A.B.Baird Publishing believe that all our writers are incredibly talented and encourage you to explore new writers often! You can find the Instagram handles for the writers listed at the front of the book.

Our goals here at A.B.Baird Publishing center on continuing to empower writers by giving social media based authors as many avenues as possible towards publication. If you are interested in how you can become published, or want to stay up to date on our latest ventures, please join our email list on our website www.abbairdpublishing.com or visit us on instagram @a.b.baird_publishing.

Your reviews mean more to us than you realize! One of the keys to continued success is having reviews on sites such as Amazon. If you have enjoyed this anthology we as that you please let us know by leaving reviews on the amazon listing. In addition we always encourage you to check out the authors on their social media accounts and let them know what you think of their work!

Thank you for your support- without you, we would be nothing!

Austie Baird - Owner
A.B.Baird Publishing